Progress and Perils in Daily Life in Ancient Rome
An Entertaining Exploration of Roman History from the Beginning of the Republic to the Fall of the Empire

Veronica Ambrose

Progress and Perils in Daily Life in Ancient Rome: An Entertaining Exploration of Roman History from the Beginning of the Republic to the Fall of the Empire

© Copyright 2021 Bishop & Hudson

All rights reserved. No part of this publication may be reproduced, stored in a retrieval system, or transmitted, in any form or by any means, electronic, mechanical, photocopying, recording, or otherwise, without the prior written permission of the copyright owner.

ISBN epub: 978-1-949282-68-9
ISBN print book: 978-1-949282-69-6

Table of Contents

Introduction	1
Chapter 1: Latrines	4
Chapter 2: Bath Houses	14
Chapter 3 – Aqueducts, Fresh Water, and Irrigation	20
Chapter 4 – Medicine and Public Health	28
Chapter 5 – Education	45
Chapter 6 – Law and Public Order	59
Chapter 7 – Wine	72
Chapter 8 – Roadways and Travel	84
Sources and Further Reading	96

Claim Your Free Gift

To get your free e-book "Crazy Roman Cabbage Therapies" please email us at:

bishopandhudson@outlook.com

For discounts and free offers on our other publications, please search for Bishop and Hudson on Facebook, Instagram, Twitter, and YouTube.

Introduction

The question "What have the Romans ever done for us?" may be one of the most often-quoted lines from the movie *Monty Python's Life of Brian*. Played by John Cleese, the leader Reg tries to rouse his followers into action against their Roman oppressors when the group asks this well-known question.

At the end of his rant, Reg has to concede that "apart from the sanitation, the medicine, education, wine, public order, irrigation, roads, a fresh water system, and public health, what have the Romans ever done for us?" [1] The satire in the movie, not to mention the complete ludicrous tone of this dialogue in particular, make it clear that there was great progress in many areas of life in ancient Roman times.

Medical knowledge was quite advanced for its time, and the ancient Romans really did make improvements in many areas of human life. They're known for developing public water and sewage systems, for their use of aqueducts, and for erecting a huge drainage system called the Cloaca Maxima. So as Roman rule spread to the edge of the European continent and beyond over the centuries, it brought with it government, public improvements, and just good plain civilization.

If you're a fan of all things related to our great toga-wearing ancestors, you probably already know that the ancient city of Rome was established in 753 BC. The Roman Kingdom existed from that time until 509 BC, when the last king was overthrown and the Roman Republic was established.

The Republic had its ups and downs through the centuries, but it came to an end between 31 and 27 BC when the ruler Octavian rose to prominence and gained the title Augustus. This transition marked the end of the Roman Republic and established the beginning of the Roman Empire.

So when we refer to the Roman Empire in this book, we are going to be talking about the later days of ancient Rome when things were more developed, from 27 BC when Caesar Augustus came into power until 476 AD, when the last Roman emperor, Romulus Augustulus, was deposed and the empire fell. In total then, we are going to be describing the period from 753 BC to around 1200 years later when Roman rule had ended.

We're going to have an entertaining, and sometimes irreverent, look at all the progress made in Roman sanitation, medicine, education, wine, public order, irrigation, roads, the fresh water system, and public health in this book, as well as looking at some of the perils or downsides of these advances in civilization. So, let's start off with a look at one of the most essential aspects of Roman civilization: the toilet.

Chapter 1 – Latrines

If the truth be told, Roman toilets were actually a bit disgusting. Water did not run directly into most households. So, the Romans built a public system of toilets starting during the time of the Roman Republic in the second century BC. The Romans called these public toilets "rooms of easement." Interestingly, the word "easement" in this is expression is normally understood to refer to the convenience or ease of access to the public toilet, rather than in the sense of easing or relieving oneself.

While the toilets were convenient, they were definitely not as private and comfortable as they are for us nowadays. Most public toilets were called latrines, and basically, they were communal toilets or just simple outhouses. The communal experience consisted of rectangular platforms that had several seats right next to one another. More often than not, there could be as many as twenty other users just on one side of these latrine blocks, and they usually had toilets on two or three sides, so they could be crowded places.

You can forget about five-foot-high cubicles like we have in modern restrooms and public toilets. There were occasionally small privacy partitions in some communal toilets in those days, but most of them simply went without this extravagance. And these communal latrine rooms were often shared by users of any gender.

The toilets themselves were considered very advanced for their time, though. The toilet seats were hand-crafted by carving openings in slabs of stone. Water from the Roman aqueduct ran constantly in stone-carved troughs that were situated beneath the latrine seats. So, once "business" had been taken care of, the idea was that the waste would simply be rinsed away.

Speaking of the latrines, you most certainly have heard the expression "Don't get the wrong end of the stick." Did you know that this expression comes from the Roman toilet? In order to cleanse oneself after visiting the latrine, the user would employ a utensil called a *tersorium*. Sounds fancy doesn't it? But it was basically a sponge on a stick.

If you have a nervous or queasy disposition, you should turn away now . . . because the sponge on the stick was also used communally – and it was only rinsed in water between users. Now, imagine, if you happened to grab this implement by the sponge before it had been rinsed. Well, then you well and truly had gotten the wrong end of the stick. Users should have been apprehensive about using the *tersorium* for other reasons too. Research today has shown that these shared sponges were the primary culprit in spreading diseases like typhoid and cholera.

Other factors also meant that visiting the latrine may not have been totally safe and acceptably sanitary, if not a bit perilous. Fires sometimes burned from the seats of Roman latrines due to the combustion of noxious gases. Unaware of the actual cause of these fires, Romans simply ascribed them to the work of demons. So, it wasn't uncommon to see incantations such as "abracadabra" written on the walls of the latrine. The goddess of good fortune, Fortuna, was also replied upon for a safe visit to the latrine. Visitors to the latrine would appeal to her to avert a fire tickling their cheeks as they sat down, as well as just to have a satisfactory outcome while using the toilet. [2]

As if all this wasn't enough to put off a visit to public conveniences, there were also other perils. As sometimes happens, users would fail to gauge their aim correctly on occasion, so urine and feces could end up on the floor and on other surfaces in the latrine.

It was actually really significant when latrine surfaces were on brown alert. That's because research has shown that the Roman population was riddled with parasites. Where did this evidence come from? Well, some scientists had the unenviable task of analyzing ancient fossilized poop. According to this evidence, worms seemed to be the most prevalent digestive complaint, apart from dysentery, so having tapeworm, roundworm, or whipworm was a very common experience.

These scientists also discovered that worms were passed from food sources and through food mishandling. The Romans just loved a fish sauce called garum, but the problem was that this condiment usually contained tapeworms. Of course, the Romans didn't have refrigeration in those days, so the garum was kept at room temperature. This atmosphere was a perfect breeding ground for tapeworms and bacteria, and since garum was such a popular condiment – used like mayonnaise or ketchup today – many people had tapeworms. [3]

All worms in the human body are passed out via the posterior, and anyone who came into contact with these contagions in the latrines would get them on their hands, and then go on to spread the problem. This problem went on for several centuries in ancient Rome. In the first century AD, Galen, a famous doctor that we'll look at a bit later, observed and described the three different kinds of intestinal worms. Unfortunately, however, he believed that worms came about because of imbalances in the body. So, even though the Imperial Romans eventually understood that worms existed, there was no reason to connect them with poor sanitation practices since they thought they originated within, rather than outside, the human body.

With all of these intestinal worms lurking around, you might think that it was just as well then that there was usually a basin for handwashing after visitors to the latrines had finished "taking care of business." But although soap existed during this time, it was not widely used, and rinsing one's hands off with water after using the latrine was certainly not ideal hand-hygiene.

There were many latrines in Rome and other Roman cities, and all of this wastewater from these public latrines had to be removed somehow. So, the sewage and wastewater payload from the public latrines went into sewers beneath the cities. The sewer in the city of Rome deserves special mention here since it really was a grand sewer. In the 6th century BC, this great sewer, called the Cloaca Maxima, was built by Roman engineers. The construction began during the reign of Tarquinius Priscus, who was one of the last kings of Rome.

The Cloaca Maxima was originally built as was an open drainage system. It was almost twenty feet wide and extended over many miles. Surprisingly, its original purpose wasn't for sewage. Its initial function was to manage water from the marshlands and low-lying areas and to carry storm water away from the city to protect the Forum and other parts of Rome.

After construction had finished on it, parts of this open drain were covered, and eventually the entire sewer was underground. It was at this point that the wastewater from the latrines started to be emptied into the system. Under these circumstances, life in ancient Rome did get a bit smelly, but the Romans did try to minimize the odors. They attempted to remove all of the sewage waste from the city with the continuous flow of water from aqueducts, which we'll look at a bit later.

Suffice it to say for now that the population of Rome and its territories really exploded during the height of the Empire. To cope with this problem, the Romans built more and more aqueducts. By the end of the first century AD, for example, there were eleven aqueducts in Rome, and all of these were channeled to the sewers. Nevertheless, the human body on average passes out about a pound and a half of waste each time a number two is produced. With a million people in Rome in the fifth century AD, that's nearly 750 tons of fecal matter being produced per day.

Little wonder that research shows that the pressure of the water from the aqueducts wasn't really sufficient to cope with the volume of waste being produced. This meant that a lot of the smelly stuff wasn't actually washed away.

Still, a good amount of foul water was coming from all of these public latrines. So, where did this all of this sewage end up? Considered to be a convenient solution for its time, the public sewer emptied into the Tiber River in Rome, which flows to the Mediterranean Sea, so this was certainly not ideal for ecology.

Archeology has revealed that some households in Ancient Rome did have private toilets, but these toilets weren't connected to the public water supply. People it seems were put off by the expense, the unreliability of the pipes, and the fear of potential fires, as well as the presence of the dreaded Roman toilet rat.

These private toilets were made up of one stone seat, and the waste was held in a container below. You might think this sounds a little bit better than a public latrine. However, the problem was that these private toilets were usually situated right next to the cooking area in the kitchen, so this was certainly not ideal for food hygiene.

What happened to the contents of the containers from these private toilets, you may well ask? Well, that was sometimes a case of "waste not, want not" rather than a case of the waste not being wanted. In fact, many Romans really knew the value of this "brown gold." Those who had the means and connections to do so would either sell it to farmers as fertilizer or use it on plants in their own gardens.

You may already know that human and animal waste is still used as fertilizer in many countries around the world today. It is certainly an economical and eco-friendly thing to do. It is good for plants and the planet and can be good for the health in general, but the waste first needs to be composted for long enough to kill off any parasites or eggs that are present in it. Without the benefit of the microscope, the ancient Romans did not realize this. As a result, the practice of fertilization was also spreading germs and parasites.

So, that was how sanitation was handled in the latrines and in some of the private households in ancient Rome. It's well known that in Rome, like in London and many other ancient cities, waste would sometimes be dumped out of household windows and onto the streets, even after the latrines had come to town. This was clearly unsanitary since it increased the likelihood of members of the public being exposed to germs and other organisms.

This practice did dramatically diminish after the latrines were constructed but, like in any society, there are just going to be those who don't stick to the so-called norms or expectations, and the ancient Romans were no exception. Since many people consider ancient Rome to have been quite advanced for its time, it might surprise you that the dumping of human waste from chamber pots took place with a particular regularity.

Obviously, something had to be done about this situation, so by the first century AD, the Romans started to pass laws that levied fines against those fouling the streets and requiring cities to remove any waste from public areas. Yet, this measure may have done more harm than good. The waste that was removed from the streets, as well as the brown gold that was being used for fertilizer, was actually causing germs to become airborne. On the whole then, it's more than likely that any street-cleaning that was done led to infection or re-infection of a large section of the population.

So, even though the presence of latrines and toilet related-sanitation in ancient Rome and its territories may have improved public hygiene to a certain extent, we probably need to stop short of saying that they were a real benefit to the health of the Romans. Yet, in spite of its pro's and con's, Rome's sewage system was more advanced and developed compared to others. In fact, this sewer served Rome from the time of the Republic, through the Empire, and up until three hundred years ago, and today, it's still used to carry storm water away from the city. [4]

Chapter 2 – Bath Houses

We've had a look at latrines and wastewater, but that's only part of the progress that was made in sanitation in ancient Rome. Bath houses began to be built during the time of the Roman Republic, at the end of the third century BC. More bath houses continued to be built over time, especially during the days of the Empire. In Rome itself, for instance, there were 170 small bath houses in the city in 33 BC, but this grew to 856 bath houses by the end of the Empire in the fifth century AD. [5]

While the wealthiest Romans would certainly have had bathing facilities in their villas, many Romans preferred to bathe in a communal setting, so they used the public bath houses for this purpose. These public bath houses were usually situated on garden squares, with the latrines being on one side and the bath houses on the other. In order to operate bath houses, huge amounts of water were needed. For this reason, some aqueducts were built just to provide water to the baths [5].

The bath houses really were progressive for their time. They had more latrines within them, and as early as the second century BC, they were heated. The heating was accomplished by lighting fires below the floor to heat the up the water that was situated there. This made the bath houses warm, comfortable places. Moreover, it was inexpensive to get in. So, going to the bath became a normal part of daily life for many Romans.

In terms of how these bath houses progressed over time, men and women had separate bathing facilities during the time of the Roman Republic, but in the early part of the Roman Empire, around the first century AD, mixed bathing became common practice. Since you might have your slave in attendance to help you while you bathed, there were separate entrances for men, women, and slaves. Once inside, you could socialize, play games, and converse while you cleaned yourself up.

So, we know that the ancient Romans were concerned about personal cleanliness and health, and they believed that good health came from regular massage, bathing, and exercise – but especially bathing. The average ancient Roman could bathe several times during the week. In other words, they really refused to rest on their *laurels* when it came to bathing!

During the time of the Empire, as the Romans conquered new territories, they increasingly discovered areas that had natural hot springs. These were called *termae*, from the Latin word for thermal, and they were ideal for baths. We know that there were several hot springs like this near Rome and Sicily, as well as in Tuscany, and even as far afield as the city of Bath in England. The baths built around these hot springs were more elaborate affairs than the standard bath house, but of course, hot springs weren't widely available. So, where there were no hot springs nearby, communal baths continued to be used and were supplied water from the nearest aqueduct.

All of these communal baths were all laid out along very similar lines, and they remained this way throughout the centuries. Basically, they consisted of four chambers. First, the bather would enter the changing room to undress, and they might even have had a couple of their slaves there to assist with their clothing and personal items. After disrobing, they would enter the tepidarium or warm room. They considered this a place just to relax for a little bit before going into the next chamber.

The next chamber was the caldarium, or hot room. Slaves were usually present in this chamber too. They would rub oil over the body of their owner, especially olive oil, which was a popular commodity. Such was the demand for olive oil in those days, that an entire mountain was formed out of the fragments of the used pots that were dumped there. Known as *Monte Tescaccio*, but also by the alternative name *Monte dei Cocci* – which means the mountain of shards – this huge mound is located right beside the ancient port on the Tiber River and can still be seen today.

So, the use of olive oil was really widespread, and once applied to the body in the baths, they would scrape off the oil, as well as any dirt and sweat, with a tool called a strigil. The strigil was a small curved metal blade-like implement that was used to scrape the skin. Once oiled and scraped, Romans would sit in the hot, steamy caldarium for a while and sweat it out with their friends.

It's kind of important to point out here that in Roman times, especially during the time of the Empire, the majority of the bathers would probably have been male. This is a significant fact because a lot of business deals were done in the public baths. The communal, and therefore social, aspect of the baths made them great places to do business, especially in the caldarium, which was where bathers were most relaxed.

Finally, the bathers would go to the frigidarium, which was a cold bath, where they could swim. This would provide the all-important exercise segment of the health-inducing massage-bathing-exercise regime. You'd need to have your slave on standby here again. Because once you got out of the frigidarium, your slave – if you had the financial means to afford one – would anoint your body with perfumed oils. Botanical fragrances like jasmine, lavender, rose, violet, camphor, and clove were used alongside animal-based scents, like musk from deer and ambergris from the sperm whale. In addition, scented powders were made with talc, and they were carried in sachets or sewn into garments.

Having read these facts, you could be forgiven for thinking that the average Roman smelled great and was squeaky clean. But while some ancient Romans may have smelled like perfume, the evidence doesn't seem to support the conclusion about cleanliness. In fact, inventions like the baths and the strigil might have made things less sanitary.

Like the latrines, those nasty little creepy-crawlies were the main peril in bath houses. Remember those scientists who examined the fossilized poop? Well, they also had a look at personal items collected from ancient Roman baths – things like fabrics and combs. In addition to again revealing evidence of the ubiquitous presence of worms, these items showed that Romans also had lice and fleas.

How could these infections have become so prominent if people were bathing regularly, you may wonder? Well, everybody shared the same water in the public bath, and this water wasn't changed with any great frequency. Also, the oils that were used as fragrances, as well as substances from other natural cosmetics, would end up in the water. Besides this, you might have even been sharing your bath water with somebody who had an open wound.

In this kind of biological ecosphere then, a not-so-fine sheen of human filth would build up on the surface of the bath water. Apart from this, don't forget that the buildings which housed the baths were comfortably heated. So the heat, combined with the toxic human slime on the surface of the water, created the perfect breeding ground for all sorts of bacteria and unpleasantness. All in all, just as in the case of the public latrines, using the public baths was a mixed blessing, and the progress in this area of life brought with it perils and negative health consequences to the ancient Romans.

Chapter 3 – Aqueducts, Fresh Water, and Irrigation

Now we know how water was used in the latrines and bath houses. But how was this water supplied to Rome and other cities? To understand the water supply, we first need to take a look at how water arrived at its final destinations. As an example, let's look at the water supply to the city of Rome.

For over 500 years, from 312 BC up until 226 AD, aqueduct systems were being built in and around Rome. These aqueducts were constructed using bridge-like structures that were made up of a series of round stone arches that sat on top of pillars. Water from these aqueducts was distributed via pipes, tunnels, and canals, and the natural fall of the landscape and the force of gravity did most of the work in moving the water along.

For Rome, water from the Tiber River was initially used throughout the city for drinking and irrigation, and later on, to supply latrines, baths, and public fountains. After many years of use, though, it became evident that the Tiber, as well as the wells and springs around it, were not going to be adequate to meet the high water-usage demands of Rome. It didn't take the Romans long to work out another reason why using rivers as a water source wasn't going to be feasible. That was because of all of the human waste and debris that was being dumped into them. Hence, the need to build more aqueducts. So, by the first century BC, the water for aqueducts was coming from wells and structures called infiltration galleries. [6]

When most people think of aqueducts they think of the arcades, those beautiful bridge-like structures with arches, so it might surprise you to discover that most of the actual work done by the aqueducts was located underground. From the aqueduct, the water would flow into large enclosed storage tanks first of all. The ancient Romans had observed that this would give any mineral deposits or other sediments in the water a chance to settle to the bottom of the tank. After this, the water would flow out of the storage via canals and pipes. From there, the water would spread out like a spider web, going into the latrines and bath houses, or to fountains and homes by the way of more storage tanks and then more pipes. These pipes were made of two materials: clay and lead. [7]

The problem with the clay pipes was that they were relatively unreliable and could break easily. The Romans didn't really see that there was any problem with the lead pipes, apart from them being more expensive to construct, since they didn't have any knowledge of poisoning by heavy metals such as lead in those days.

Of course, we know now that exposure to lead is extremely damaging to human physical and mental health, but the Romans were blissfully unaware of these perils, and relied on lead for many of their pipes. Just to give you some idea of how much lead the Romans were exposed to in those days, research has revealed that a pipe that was around a mile in length could contain nearly five hundred pounds of lead. [8]

So, this was how water was supplied in general to infrastructures, but how did the average member of society access their own fresh water in ancient Rome? To understand this part of the equation, we first need to look at the way ancient Romans lived. That's because different members of the public would have had different water privileges depending upon their wealth and social position.

It was actually very uncommon for private Roman citizens to have a direct water supply, even if they were wealthy. To do so, the homeowner would have had to get approval from the authorities by having their plumbing inspected. And where water was supplied directly, it would have only been available on the floors at street level since the system was powered by gravity. Because of the relative unavailability of a direct water supply and due to the distances of fountains from most types of accommodation, those who could have afforded it would have had slaves to fetch and carry their water.

Life for the average Roman – in other words, those who weren't either very rich or very poor – was not lived in houses, though, but in apartment complexes called *insulae*. These complexes were normally six or seven stories in height, and the street level would have been occupied by merchants such as sellers of food, clothing, or other goods.

Families that were more well-off would have lived in the lower floors of these *insulae*. They would have multi-room apartments and would often be working as merchants. There was truly a pecking order in these types of accommodation, because the higher the floor, the poorer you were. Examining the living conditions, we can see that this is where the true perils come in. Generally, the *insulae* were poorly built. On the very top floors, there were usually no windows, so light and ventilation were very poor, making these rooms especially dank, smelly, and dark. Better that than being completely homeless though and having to sleep below an aqueduct, in a tomb, or simply under somebody's stairs, which was the experience for the poorest in Roman society.

Residents of these dismal upper-floor apartments had to carry their water up several flights of stairs and store it in their living spaces. It's known that a lot of this water was used for sanitary purposes like washing and cleaning, rather than for drinking. So, the Romans would take their buckets and pots to the fountains, fill them up, and then store them in their apartments to be used later on. In addition, you would have a chamber pot in your room for those urgent needs in the nighttime.

But don't forget that many of the fountains were built just out of a sense of sheer opulence, rather than practicality, so many of the fountains in ancient Rome were designed really to be more of a statement of the power and wealth of the Roman rulers, instead of having been built with the welfare of the masses in mind. Nevertheless, many of the other fountains were public and could be freely accessed to obtain drinking water. Within Rome itself, a public fountain could normally be found within fifty yards from any business or dwelling at the height of the Empire. However, carrying a couple of buckets of water fifty yards and then up several flights of stairs could hardly have been considered convenient.

So, the average Roman lived in these apartments. In comparison to the homes of their wealthier counterparts, who lived in villas and had a pool in which their slaves collected water for them, the sanitation and conditions in these dwellings would have been substandard, to say the least. In addition, there were no kitchens or cooking facilities in most rooms. Not surprising then that most tenants in ancient Rome would have spent most of their time outside of their dwellings, dining on cheap food in taverns and using their rooms really only for sleep. [9] On the whole then, there were a few negative effects on their quality of life, not to mention the inconvenience involved in water access and storage for these apartment dwellers.

You might not be amazed then to discover that it was commonplace to attempt to bribe water officials for better water access. But bribery sometimes didn't do the trick, so the practice of puncturing also sprang into existence. For this to take place, the main water pipe would be secretly accessed – in other words, punctured – and a new pipe would be laid without permission in order to provide a direct supply of water to a business or dwelling. Of course, this practice was completely illegal, so it was part of the job of water officials to check for secret networks of pipes such as these. After all, direct access to the water supply was intended primarily for the latrines, the bath house, and the fountains, not to mention those really rich Romans who lived in their own homes.

So, we've had a look at how water was supplied and used in urban settings. However, part of the water supply also needed to be used in rural settings for irrigation if the population was going to be fed. In rural settings, irrigation systems would vary slightly depending on geology. As a result, this is probably where the ingenuity of the ancient Romans may have been the most evident. Many different irrigation problems were encountered, and the Romans learned how to develop rather complex strategies for dealing with them. No surprise then that the high demand for water in urban life, along with the complexity of supplying water for rural demands, meant that some controls were needed.

Legislation was eventually developed to regulate water usage and protect the rights of users. Later on, we'll have a look at how many Roman so-called rights, like water rights, could be used as a political tool for rulers, who often used them to control the populace.

So again, we find that the use of bath houses, as well as public access to water for both urban and rural users, came with both advantages and disadvantages. Because of the presence of lead in the water supply and the inconvenience of transporting water for personal use, the quality of life in ancient Roman society would have suffered to a certain extent, especially for the poorest.

Chapter 4 – Medicine and Public Health

Thus far we've encountered a few perils associated with life in ancient Rome. With there being lead in the water supply and with hygiene in the latrines and bath houses not being the greatest, the health of the average Roman might have suffered somewhat. So, to deal with the basic human need of good health, the Romans developed many medical practices, both during the time of the Republic, as well as during the Empire.

In the early days of ancient Rome, healing consisted mainly of rituals. The Romans in those days believed that many diseases had supernatural causes, so many of their so-called remedies were based on magic. The Romans, like the Greeks, believed in the theory of the four humors: earth, air, fire, and water. If you were suffering from an imbalance of the four humors, you would first be prescribed a regime of diet, activity, exercise, and bathing to rebalance the humors. That doesn't sound too bad so far, does it? However, woe betide the person who failed to respond appropriately to these therapies.

If the diet-activity-exercise-bathing solution failed to work, the next course of action was normally blood-letting. If that failed, it would then be time to administer hellebore, a potent poison. Once this terrible tincture was administered, the patient would have fits of vomiting and diarrhea. The plentiful purging of these pungent bodily fluids was a great sign, which indicated that the victim – or rather patient – had eliminated the imbalance in their humors, and they would be deemed cured.

The ancient Romans also believed that certain stones had healing powers, a belief that is still shared by New Age practitioners today. The stones were especially helpful if worn as amulets or charms. For instance, aquamarine was used to remedy sea-sickness, the green jasper stone was believed to ward off evil spirits and bring balance to one's life, and the okytokia stone was worn by expectant mothers to bring about a quick childbirth.

The Romans began to move towards something more like conventional medicine around 200 BC. Actually, it was in 219 BC, during the time of the Roman Republic, that the first Greek physician arrived in Rome from the Peloponnese. The arrival of this Greek doctor, whose name was Archagathus, was recorded by a Roman author called Pliny the Elder for short, but whose real name was the much fancier Latin-based Gaius Plinius Secundus.

Pliny describes how Archagathus would cut and then burn the flesh of those who had ironically turned to the physician for healing. These actions earned Archagathus the title of "carnifex," which is Latin for the butcher. Soon, other self-proclaimed "physicians" began to travel to Rome from Greece. This was truly bad news, so of course, the Roman elders had to decide what to do about the situation. Another Roman elder called Cato started to spread the word around that there was some sort of Greek conspiracy. The lowdown according to Cato was that the Greeks had sent these butchers to Rome as revenge for the Roman conquest during the Macedonia Wars.

Despite these traditionalists' distrust in them, Greek physicians did become extremely popular over time. In fact, Greek doctors were once so highly-regarded that both Roman Emperors Caesar and Augustus granted them Roman citizenship, which effectively meant that they could never go back to Greece. In time, of course, the Romans began to educate themselves in what they considered to be the art of medicine, and this was based on what they had observed from the Greeks.

The net result of this culture of self-education was that there was no real formal training in the art of medicine. In those days, anyone could proclaim that they were a doctor and could open a clinic without any experience or expertise. Because of this, the remedies employed by these physicians in those days ranged from the sublime to the ridiculous.

As the practice of medicine expanded during the time of the Republic, Roman physicians became increasingly involved in the use of herbs, spices, and plants. While fennel, garlic, fenugreek, egg yolk, boiled liver, and cabbage might sound like an outlandish menu for a nightmarish dinner invitation in our day and age, the Romans used each and every one of these ingredients as medicines.

Fennel was used for general healing, as well as for nervous disorders, garlic for the heart, and fenugreek for the lungs. Perhaps most counter-intuitive was that raw egg yolk, which we often associate with salmonella and digestive discomfort, was used as a cure for dysentery. The boiled liver in our aforementioned delightful dinner-party menu would be applied over the eyes, to help with soreness and to promote healing.

Since it was so widely used in medicine, cabbage deserves its own special mention. This brassicaceous beauty was really regarded as a kind of wonder cure of its age, and during the second century BC, Cato the

Elder recommended it for an abundance of everyday discomforts and maladies. Got a hangover? Why not drink a bit of cabbage water? Digestive troubles? Eat half a cabbage to make it worse before it gets better. Trying to get pregnant? Well, then boil a cabbage and direct the fumes from the water into the lady's intimate area. Got a wound or open sore? First apply a cabbage leaf, followed by some unwashed wool.

If these remedies failed to work, then it was time to up the game. Using "pre-processed" cabbage was often believed to be better than the fresh stuff. So, how was it pre-processed, you may well ask? Well, it was consumed as food and then the urine of those who ate it was collected to be used to bathe others. One of Cato's most widely-used purposes of this cabbage urine was for newborns. He believed that bathing the baby in the urine of a large consumer of cabbage was extremely advantageous to the constitution and the general health of the infant.

Chamomile, which was used as a flatulence remedy, may have been needed by those who had consumed this all-important but gas-inducing leafy vegetable. Apart from this, patients who had been on the receiving end of the urine-based remedy endorsed by Cato may have really needed willow, which was used as an antiseptic.

There was also the mysterious silphium, which was believed to be a kind of large fennel. Silphium was used as a contraceptive, but also for other remedies – for complaints ranging from sore throat to coughs and fever, as well as for indigestion and warts.

So, what happened when these cabbage-based remedies turned out to be ineffective? Well, it was time to bring back a little bit of magic, of course. Those who failed to respond to cabbage therapy would have had to recite tongue-twisting incantations, such as "motas uaeta daries dardaries" or "asiadarides una te pes" in order to be cured. [10]

Besides the physicians of the day, Roman medicine was also administered by the *pater familias*, which translates from Latin as the father of the house. The pugnacious patriarch would cure his family by employing wine, oil, and again, wool that was unwashed.

Perhaps because treatments like these were not only unreliable, but often left the patient worse off than before, Cato the Elder ultimately proclaimed that illness should be considered a test of character. In his view, a person demonstrated great strength and valiance if they managed to overcome sickness after using the remedies found in nature. [11]

As the practice of medicine grew, it also became an extremely profitable enterprise, and those who practiced it were able to make money very easily. But physicianship and the fledgling medical profession in general were still unregulated activities during the time of the Republic at least. Little wonder that this high-profit, low-regulation phenomenon created the perfect storm, and as a result, a number of shady characters began to be associated with the practice of medicine.

Not surprisingly, an atmosphere like this produced some outright charlatans who had no real interest in healing or even helping people, and many entirely-unsuitable and ill-equipped members of society, such as weavers, cobblers, and tanners, became fly-by-night medical practitioners. The on-the-job training for these former main-street merchants consisted merely of practicing and learning by experimenting directly on their patients, including cutting open their skin.

Later on, as the Empire was established and expanded, things did become a little bit better, and doctors were starting to get something like professional training. Nonetheless, doctors who actually received training were only really a little better off. For instance, the doctor Thessalus, who practiced during Emperor Nero's government in the first century AD, is known for bragging that his medical training lasted for six whole months.

Throughout the Republic and the Empire, the most highly-valued physicians were able to achieve very high incomes in ancient Rome. They gained money not only through the often-inflated fees they charged for their services, but also through gifts that were given to them. Because if you were rich in ancient Rome, you wanted everyone to know about it, and what better way to publicize your wealth and new-found health than by gifting your doctor a valuable asset, or just good old cash, once you'd recovered from your illness.

However, it doesn't take a genius to work out what happened next. Some physicians got greedy. Yes, they acted against the very few ethics that then existed in the practice of medicine. They prolonged expensive or even unnecessary treatments. They started to demand huge fees for cheap medicines, and some were even so bold as to kill their patients if they knew that a bequest was going to be made to them in the patient's will.

One of the most well-regarded physicians in ancient Rome was Galen, who was originally from Greece. Galen acted as the personal physician to many of Rome's most famous emperors over several decades, but somewhat shockingly, by the end of the second century AD, Galen pointed out that many of his so-called colleagues couldn't even read. Perhaps because of Galen's protests against the untrained in the profession, some of the most ignorant and lethal doctors were eventually put on trial.

Let's turn our thoughts now to the specialisms that many of our doctors practice nowadays. In contrast, doctors in ancient Rome normally didn't specialize in any particular branch of medicine during the time of the Republic. Later on though, some of the larger cities in the Roman Empire did begin to welcome medical specialists in fields such as surgery, ophthalmology, and otorhinolaryngology, which we know today by the much simpler abbreviation ENT.

Perhaps somewhat alarmingly, gynecology was not widely considered to be a special branch of medicine in those days. Midwives delivered more babies than did gynecologists, and a doctor would be called to attend a woman in labor only if there were obvious complications. Caesarean deliveries, said to be named after the great Julius Caesar himself, did sometimes take place, but while the woman would not survive the procedure, the baby just might.

When other surgery was performed, the patent would not receive anesthesia. Instead, patients undergoing surgical procedures would receive something equivalent to today's narcotics. Natural ingredients like poppy juice and the autumn crocus, which contained morphine and colchicine, were widely used, but opium and scopolamine were used more often. Narcotics like these would relieve pain and numb the senses of the patient. In the meantime, hapless surgeons' assistants were required to hold down when the patient while the doctor operated on them. Afterwards, they would continue to hold down the patient as they applied acid vinegar to clean up the patients' surgical wounds.

Since they did not have effective anesthetics for surgical procedures, Imperial Roman surgeons were unable to perform complicated operations like we have today, so surgery was probably limited to the surface of the body in most cases. However, some medical instruments did exist during this time, and more complicated operations and procedures were carried out. These operations included the examination of the lower bowel, the removal of cataracts, trephination, which consisted of drilling a hole in the skull to reveal the brain, and even the reversal of circumcision. So, that involves operations on the eyes, the brain, and a gentleman's delicate parts.

What could possibly have gone wrong? And getting to the bottom line, how did they inspect the lower bowel? With an anal speculum, of course. As it turned out, the Roman tool for rectal examination was a pretty important invention. In fact, we still use an updated version of it today.

When surgery was needed, incisions were closed with flax, linen thread, or even metal pins. Dressings consisted of linen bandages or sponges, which could be used either dry for absorption, or wet, having been soaked in wine, oil, vinegar, or water and having kept hydrated during surgery by being covered with a garland of fresh leaves.

So, how did the Romans obtain all of this knowledge about surgery? Well, the answer may be more practical, but also more gruesome, than you could have imagined. As Roman rule expanded during the time of the Empire, increasing numbers of soldiers were required to conquer new domains and keep them under control, so the Romans needed to keep their soldiers in the best possible running order. To help achieve this goal, they developed surgical tools to be used on the battlefield. A common procedure was the removal of arrowheads, but they also performed other necessary procedures to save and protect the valuable lives of their soldiers.

On the battlefield, Roman surgeons carried a sort of medical tool kit. It held things like arrowhead extractors, scalpels, forceps, and catheters. They knew that their tools should be as sterile as possible, so they sterilized their equipment in boiling water before each procedure. Roman surgeons also knew that veins and arteries contained blood and helped it travel around the body, so they were trained in the use of things like tourniquets and clamps to limit the flow of blood.

But let's get to the more perilous, truly gruesome part. Although some of these medical procedures were advanced for their time, there was of course a limit to what could be done in ancient Roman times, and amputations happened with a certain gruesome frequency. The Romans new that gangrene and ultimately lethal sepsis would set in unless this drastic action was taken. Here, we see the use of one of the more important surgical tools: the bone saw.

So, after this surgery was done, patients would simply be left to recover the best they could, and very little was actually done to promote and restore health. Without the benefit of the microscope, surgeons in those days would have been unaware of the changes that can occur on a cellular level to promote healing. Nor would they have understood anything as sophisticated as germ theory.

Yet, through observation, they did realize that within two weeks, a callus would form on the end of the amputated shaft and that this would normally smooth over with new skin.

It might also be a surprise to learn that the Romans developed prosthetics. For example, prosthetic legs have been discovered in tombs in southern Italy. That particular prothesis, which could be considered an example for others that might have existed, consisted of a leg made of wood and covered in bronze, which was attached to a leather and bronze belt. [12]

In the observations of health and medicine on the battlefield, Romans also understood that barracks should be placed well away from swampy or wet areas. And if wetlands got in the way of their military plans, they would simply drain the swamp. The Romans had observed the link between bodies of water and mosquitoes, and they knew that these insects were capable of transmitting certain diseases to humans. This awareness of mosquitoes and disease from the battlefield didn't generally translate well to the public, however, especially to those living in Rome. Disease, particularly malaria, was widespread in Rome during the later days of the Empire, and this was simply due to the fact that the city had become so overcrowded.

Getting back to medical knowledge from the battlefield, doctors within the Roman army were able to do their best because the military "machine" was organized. More importantly, they were careful about being secretive about any new procedures or techniques that they had discovered, so they could share their medical knowledge throughout the Roman Empire without their enemies finding out. As mentioned before, they were seriously motivated by the death and wounding of their soldiers, although more from a perspective of protecting soldiers as assets, rather than any feelings of humanity for them.

So, did Roman society benefit from all of this war, death, and destruction? Well, yes, it actually did. Through their observations on the battlefield, Roman doctors began to appreciate the importance of public health, and as Roman doctors acquired knowledge on the battlefield, benefits started to accrue to Roman society at large. Unlike their Greek counterparts, however, Roman doctors were forbidden by law from dissecting human corpses, and this did create certain limitations in their understanding of human anatomy.

The famous second century physician Galen got around this problem by performing dissections on animals, especially apes. Through these observations, Galen was able to understand bone structure and anatomy in great depth. It was also the through observation of the consequences of cutting the spinal cord of one of his specimens that Galen realized that the brain sends signals to the body which control the muscles. In this way, Galen's understanding of anatomy was based primarily on animal dissections, which he then used to interpret human anatomy.

His first studies in human anatomy were gained when he was a gladiators' surgeon. Imagine the delight that one with an inquiring mind would experience as he stared into gaping wounds suffered in combat. In so doing, Galen was able to observe the internal structure of the human body. He was able to gain unsurpassed anatomical knowledge through these observations, so much so that he was considered to be the expert on human anatomy during his time.

Besides learning about anatomy, the Imperial Romans also progressed in understanding what caused disease in general, and they learned how they could prevent certain illnesses. Some of their medical theories even resembled those of today. For example, in the first century BC, Marcus Terentius Varro claimed that disease happened because of small creatures that were too tiny to be seen by the human eye. Unfortunately, others still believed that bad smells or vapors caused disease, and others hung onto the belief that the stars or supernatural forces were what caused illness and disease.

With all of this knowledge and experience behind them, the Romans ultimately developed a system of hospitals. Ever practical, Romans initially established hospitals inside forts, but then expanded them to the civilian population. Roman military hospitals, like the one discovered in Chester, England, had small rooms situated off of a long corridor or around a courtyard. These military hospitals were then later used to take care of the sick in general, rather than those wounded in battle.

Hospitals developed even further when the Romans erected new buildings especially for that purpose. The goal of these new structures was to provide a place where the ill and injured could be treated and rest and recover. In the hospital setting, Roman doctors were able to observe the sick and dying further, which helped to advance their knowledge of how to diagnose and treat conditions. Roman doctors also began to perform routine physical examinations on their patients.

But perhaps because of the egos sometimes involved, different doctors would develop conflicting theories, and treatment could sometimes go off track into several different directions. On a practical level, all of this meant that the diagnosis and treatment of disease and illness in ancient Rome was in reality a very inconsistent, patchy, and sometimes perilous business at best.

Chapter 5 – Education

Just as medical care developed under Roman rule, so too did education. The education of young children, in particular, was central to the Roman educational system. Before considering the education of children though, we should first have a look at the dichotomy in how children from different social classes were treated in ancient Rome.

Some inhabitants of the Roman Republic and Empire would have been extremely ill-equipped to care for an infant, let alone to bring up a child. That was simply because of the financial and social limitations they faced. To put it bluntly, Roman society was supposed to be limited to members who could be economically profitable to it. So, a more-or-less accepted practice called "child exposure" existed in those days. Under this practice, those who felt that they couldn't bring up a child would simply abandon their infants in public places. Of course, this often resulted in infanticide, with the child usually dying from hypothermia or starvation.

On a cynical level, we could say that this was done merely to free the parent from the obligations of childrearing. On a more humanitarian level, it should be pointed out that many parents did this in the hope that a more affluent family would find their child and take care of it, and these parents would often leave amulets around the necks of their children as good luck charms for this very purpose. Because of this practice of child exposure, among other things, life expectancy was very poor for the youngest members of the Roman population. A staggering fifty percent of all children died before age of ten, and a third died even before reaching their first birthday.

In spite of these sad statistics, it does seem that the children who survived the perils of infancy were given the very best that their parents could offer them. Since there was such a huge emphasis on becoming a productive member of society in ancient Rome, the care, training, and education of children was also treated with a certain amount of seriousness.

So, how were these children educated? In the second century BC, the Romans conquered Greece, and at that time, they imported many Greek educational methods, in addition to many educated Greek slaves, but unlike their Greek neighbors, the Romans never set up the infrastructure for formal schooling – things like school buildings and a system of training teachers in any uniform way therefore simply didn't exist in ancient Rome.

Because of this lack of infrastructure, costs were associated with getting an education. So generally, only the wealthy would receive something like a formal education. Parents were especially concerned about the education of their children because it was the belief of many people, especially the wealthy, that children could be imbued with knowledge from the very moment of birth.

Some were concerned that their children's nurses should be as educated as possible for women of their station, so that children would not be exposed to grammatically incorrect utterances at a tender age. It was feared that children would go on to imitate incorrect grammatical forms and learn to speak improperly as a result. After all, Romans believed that habits learned at a young age, even as an infant, could be hard to break later in life. [13]

For those who could not afford a nurse, both parents were responsible for the training of their children during their early years. The bulk of this training focused on moral values though, rather than on developing the intelligence. Children were expected to be obedient to their parents and to those in authority, and their obedience was to be absolute and unquestioning. In addition, children were expected to be truthful, respectful of the law, and reverent to the Roman gods. Perhaps somewhat paradoxically, with the importance placed upon their unquestioning obedience, they were also expected to be self-sufficient and confident. In short, they were expected to be dutiful, good, and pious little Romans.

During most of a child's early life then, they were in constant contact with their parents. They would sit at the table with their parents and other elder relatives, and might even help to serve the meals. Until children were seven years old, the mother of the family served as something like a teacher in the conventional sense. She would educate her children in the early steps of the three R's: reading, writing, and basic arithmetic. They would learn things like numerals and letter and word recognition. In addition, the mother also guided her children in how to speak in a grammatically correct way in Latin, which was their first language in those days, since there was such a heavy emphasis on good elocution.

Like other aspects of ancient Roman life, a child's education depended very much on their social status and gender. After all, education then, like now, relies upon the need for certain roles within larger society. So, people tried to become as educated as they possibly could, depending of course on their social status and situation in life.

The rates of illiteracy in ancient Rome are the subject of debate. The most optimistic estimates indicate that thirty percent of the population was literate, but there also estimates as low as ten percent. And of course, there is a difference between being basically literate and being educated.

So, children from the most financially-disadvantaged homes would go without any kind of education at all. They would simply have to learn in the school of hard knocks. Aware of this harsh reality, groups of freed slaves would sometimes get together in the later days of ancient Rome as the Empire grew and offer informal classes to children from the most deprived backgrounds.

In terms of gender, most girls remained at home after the age of seven, often without much further schooling. A girl was expected to be her mother's faithful companion and to become well-versed in housekeeping and other important domestic tasks. In addition, girls from higher social classes would learn to read and write, as well as being educated in their religious rights and responsibilities. Higher-born girls might also learn the legal basics of land ownership and other financial rights, especially if they didn't have a husband. There were families who allowed their girls to take their education further than this, but this was extremely rare.

In terms of taking things further – before the next shocking fact is mentioned, it's important to point out here that life expectancy in ancient Rome was much briefer than it is for us today. This may have been one of the reasons that girls in ancient Rome could marry as young as the tender age of twelve. However, this may not be as appalling as it first seems. Evidence does seem to point out that most Roman girls were in their late teens when they married, and Roman boys, on the other hand, could marry when they were as young as fourteen.

The patriarch of the family had the right to seek useful and profitable matches for his offspring. So, daughters were expected to advance themselves by marrying into respectable families. Nevertheless, the daughter could refuse a match if she could show that her intended was of poor character.

In reality though, marriage was really built on a lopsided, skewed notion of girls and women. Females who were married weren't expected to get any enjoyment or support out of their marriages; they simply got married because it was culturally expected that they would wed and have children. Women were supposed to act subservient to their male partners, even if their husbands were unfaithful to them with a mistress – as long as the mistress herself was not married. Moreover, if her husband were so inclined, he was even permitted to have extracurricular activities with boys, as long as they were over fourteen.

With all of this subservience in mind, after a daughter's seventh birthday, mothers would teach girls about how to run a household efficiently. Part of their education would also have been in sewing, how to run a kitchen, and perhaps music. In general, girls were trained in how to be good wives, in preparation for the time when they would get married.

Being a Roman wife could actually elevate a female's status in the ancient world. That was because, ideally, a good Roman wife would be the glue that held her family together as an integrated unit. So, getting married extremely young was not without its benefits, and we can imagine that it might even have been something that some young Roman girls aspired to.

It's unclear though, what young girls might have thought about the physical obligations that came along with being a wife or if their mothers even discussed the sexual aspect of marriage with them. In our day and age, we might like to think that Roman men were chivalrous when taking a young bride and may have waited a few months or years to consummate the relationship. But again, we don't have any really consistent, *hard* evidence that this was the case!

While a girl was by educated by her mother, the boy was his father's companion. In rural settings, boys would help their fathers with farming and agricultural tasks, such as planting and tending to crops. However, rural boys would still need to be literate enough to manage the business of farming and to be able to read things like contracts and other written documents.

In urban settings, a boy would accompany his father to work in business or in his public duties, where possible. The actual instruction imparted to boys would be prone to all kinds of interruptions, though. This was particularly true for higher-born boys who had fathers in the Senate or other forms of public office. It was therefore common for these families to have a trusted slave that could help the father with the early instruction of the boys of the family. After all, slaves, especially those that were taken in combat, would often be much better educated than their owners. [14]

Upper-class boys and girls would also learn the importance of their lineage from a young age. They would be shown the busts of their ancestors and would learn the history of their family. They would also be told their parents' versions of how their family helped to influence and shape history.

Remember that any fit and well Roman male would be expected to be prepared for military action. This was true during the Republic and the Empire, but it became increasingly important as Roman rule spread across new territories during the later stages of the Empire. And even though boys might not actually join the military, being prepared to do so was important. That's because it helped boys to be courageous in the face of any danger and to assume their masculine role within society. In order to keep them fit and well, the father would teach his male offspring how to swim, box, wrestle, and ride a horse. The father would also educate his sons in how to use weapons, as well as training them in military exercises to ensure that they were combat-ready.

Something like what we would consider a formal education was the domain only of boys from better-off social classes. When these boys turned six or seven years old, they went to a private school that had teachers. In contrast, the most well-off families had tutors or educated slaves to each their own boys, and boys of neighbors or friends of the family might also be invited to these homes for their education. The slaveowner might charge the other parents a fee for these lessons, and the slave might have been able to keep part of this money, in addition to the little gifts he might get from his students.

The so-called schools that existed during the Republic and the early days of the Empire could have been anything from a curtain pulled across the back of a shop to a room in house or other building. Only very rarely would a school be an entire building that was earmarked for that purpose. Teachers in these schools might have had to embrace the concept of teaching as a vocation because they were very poorly paid and worked long hours, usually from morning to evening. In addition, the boys in these schools would range in age from six to twelve, with only one teacher for all of them.

In terms of the subjects that were taught, the boys would continue to be educated in the three R's. They improved their writing by copying words on to tablets. These tablets really were a clever invention. They consisted of two small wooden boxes that would be held together face-to-face with twine like a book. Inside each box was a layer of wax. The writing could be done into the wax with a stylus, and then the surface was smoothed over for the next use. They would learn more complex names and words, as well as some of the intricacies of writing and speaking the Latin language. They also used a special contraption to improve their arithmetic; it was a kind of calculating board that held beads – something like an abacus. [15]

At the age of eleven or twelve, boys would leave their families and progress to high school. With state-run education being non-existent in those days, getting any further education was usually something that was highly valued. This value may have been imputed to education simply because of the cost involved in getting it, and because of this cost, only the brightest children from the best families would get any further education past the age of twelve.

In the early days of the Roman Empire, sometime in the first century AD, a certain Roman educator named Quintilian rose into prominence. He claimed that schools were much better at educating children than private tutors were. Importantly, he also argued that competition between children and between schools would improve educational standards for everyone. Quintilian was quite convincing in these arguments, so during the first century AD, schools became more popular. Some fathers even thought it was prudent to spend money on educating their daughters, although the education of girls continued to be rare.

So, schools became more popular as the Empire grew. To attend a high school, children would normally need to leave home and go to live in one of the larger cities. There weren't any dormitories in those days, so their parents would need to pay for them to stay in a room with a family. The parents would also have to pay for the child's meals and other expenses, not to mention the fees for the teacher. The teachers in these high schools were educated, scholarly people known as pedagogues, who would set themselves up as schoolmasters in private houses.

Lessons would be dictated by the teacher since books as we know them weren't available in those days. When students had mastered the art of writing, they would progress from the wax tablet to paper. The paper was made from reeds of the papyrus plant, their pens were feather quills, and the ink was octopus ink.

So, single teacher would be responsible for teaching all of the *artes liberales* in high school, or what we would call the liberal arts nowadays. These included arithmetic, geometry, astronomy, grammar, logic, composition and oratory, and music. As the Empire expanded, boys from wealthier families would also be tutored in mythology, literature, philosophy, and the Greek language. After all, education of the boys from the most affluent families was supposed to develop the mental powers in order for them to be able to function in public office, in the Forum, the courts, or the Senate.

There wasn't really any choice in what subjects a student could take in a Roman high school, and boys weren't really encouraged to have critical, analytical minds. They were simply expected to memorize facts and learn things by rote. There was no real inquiry into why things were right, and with this being the case, some children must have become bored really easily. Apart from this, the school day would have been much, much longer than what we have today. Students would be expected to get up at dawn and be in class all day. They would have only a very short break for lunch, and then they would be back in their rooms by sunset in order to be rested for the next day. Perhaps most significantly, they attended class seven days a week, without any break for the weekend.

The long days, the unquestioning obedience, and the boredom must have made learning really challenging in those days. So, of course, schoolmasters needed a way to keep students in line. To achieve this goal, most learning was based on fear.

For the slightest offense, a boy would be held down by two slaves while the schoolmaster beat him with a whip or cane. Boys would be beaten for answering questions incorrectly, for being late to class, or for speaking in class without permission. As a result, students were only really motivated to learn and get things right simply because they wanted to escape punishment.

As we will see in the next chapter, this fear of punishment also came in useful in order to control the larger population. So, in the same way, fear became an integral part of law and public order in ancient Rome.

Chapter 6 – Law and Public Order

So, how was public order maintained in ancient Rome? And what laws and punishments were put in place to control an unruly populace? In order to answer these questions, we should first have a look at how the system of law and order developed from the Republic to the Empire.

In the early days of the Roman Republic, the praetor, who was the second highest in command in those days, had the job of enforcing the laws. He also administered justice through the courts. There wasn't really anything like a police force in those days, although by 27 BC, the Romans did have something called the *Vigiles*, who enforced things like theft and the capture and punishment of runaway slaves. Without a police force, the military would be deployed into action when more force was needed to control the Republic.

Laws in ancient Roman times were established by the Roman Assemblies and then voted on by citizens who were members of the assemblies. The wealthier classes, sometimes referred to as the patricians, had the majority of seats in these assemblies, but resolutions and laws were also made by the Emperor, the Senate, and the

Plebian Council – from the Latin word *pleb*, which means common person.

In terms of written law, the Romans had a constitution that the Roman government was to follow. As early as 450 BC, some of the basic laws had already been written on stones tablets called the twelve tables. However, most of the laws during the Republic weren't organized statutes like we have nowadays, because all of the laws weren't written down in one place. Later on, though, as the Empire developed, something like codified law was established through individual laws, as well as through customs and traditions.

In addition, there was a kind of legal hierarchy in family life throughout the Republic and the Empire. A concept known as *patria potestas* meant that the elder father in a line of descendants had absolute power over all of them. This power could be exerted over young children, as well as any descendant in the male side of the family, regardless of their age. So, the elder male of the family line had absolute control over his children, could treat property owned by a descendant as his own, and could even inflict capital punishment upon a descendant. Conversely, a father could free a descendant by emancipation, and with this being a patriarchal society, women could cease to be under the *patria potestas* of their fathers, but only if they instead were placed under *cum manu*, or legal control, of their husbands.

In the early days of ancient Rome, a person would be entitled to rights under Roman law only if they were a Roman citizen. During those days, there were different levels of Roman citizenship, each with different rights depending on your status, and if you weren't a Roman citizen, your protections under law would be very limited.

During the time of the Roman Republic in the second century BC, a jurist named Gaius stated quite simply that: "The main distinction in the law of persons is that all men are either free or slaves." The slave was considered a chattel, or in other words, a piece of personal property. As such, slaves had no rights or "personhood," but perhaps paradoxically, they could be held responsible for crimes and subjected to severe punishments.

When you think of slaves, you might think of those that were manual workers or those that performed domestic or personal services for their owners, but some slaves were highly skilled, performing jobs in professions such as accounting or medicine. Slavery was really very deeply embedded in ancient Roman society and was just considered a normal part of Roman life. Poor families even had slaves, and sometimes, slaves even had their owns slaves.

Later in the Empire, slaves could be freed and become Roman citizens. So, some foreigners viewed slavery as a route to Roman citizenship. They could learn a craft and the language, and so, viewed slavery as a kind of training for becoming a Roman citizen.

It is true though that many slaves were unskilled, many were treated cruelly by their masters, and many more were exploited, especially as sex slaves. Any slave would be expected to be sexually available at their master's request. Male masters could have sex with both female and male slaves, and in spite of the strict expectations on women in Roman households, it is known from archeological remains depicting the sex act that some Roman women would also have sex with male and sometimes female slaves. Interestingly, the idea of homosexuality didn't really exist in those days. There wasn't even a word in Latin to distinguish same-sex and opposite-sex desire.

While we would consider the treatment of slaves, not to mention slavery itself, to be most deplorable by our own standards, this is just how life was in those days. Slaves really had no protections at all until Emperor Nero established the right for a slave to file a complaint against a master in the first century AD.

Foreigners sometimes fared only a little better than did slaves. Since foreigners also had no rights in the early days of ancient Rome, the situation arose where Romans could seize foreigners like a piece of property, and subject them to slavery or servitude. Foreigners weren't entirely without legal protection in those days, though. As early as the middle of the third century BC, the existing nations started to develop something called *jus gentium*, which translates from Latin as the law of nations. This separate set of laws was to applied to both Romans and foreigners. You can think of it as the common law of all humankind – something like a very stripped-back version of the United Nations. The law of nations wasn't legislation; it had merely been developed by provincial governors and local magistrates, but these laws were used when justice and punishments had to be administered to foreigners. So, foreigners could receive justice and punishments, rather than having rights and protections *per se*.

It was also in the third century BC that the resolutions established by the Plebian Council, as well as the laws established by the Assemblies, became law for all classes of Roman citizens. Nevertheless, the fact that written laws were still in a somewhat disorganized state at that time, in addition to the fact that a fair amount of them were unwritten, created the perfect environment for the corruption of public officials.

The first recorded case of a Roman public official accepting a bribe was in 171 BC. In that year, a foreign diplomat did political favors for a certain Roman senator, who took handouts in exchange for his services. As sometimes happens, many people started to know about this arrangement, and the senator found that it was impossible to pay off everyone trying to blackmail him, so the news of the bribery went public. You might have thought that all of the other law-abiding Roman officials were shocked when they heard about the bribery. Of course, that was true . . . but just not how you'd think. Instead, the other officials were appalled that they weren't getting a piece of the action. And thereafter, bribery was happily accepted as standard practice in dealing with foreign officials.

At this point, the domestic politicians were feeling a bit left out, so they decided to start accepting bribes too. For example, those in the business of construction bribed senators to get their building contracts since the Senate decided who built the roads and arenas and so on.

Moreover, since the Senate made the laws, those with enough money could just pay senators to pass laws that were custom-made to suit their needs.

Then aristocrats and the wealthy joined in, using their money as bribes to get into public office in Rome. Looking to their more sophisticated urban counterparts for inspiration, the governors in the provinces also decided to join in too. After all, the governors had to look after the interests of their constituents when they reported to Rome, so it just made good sense that they would get nice little gifts, like valuable assets or cash as incentives from time to time. However, sometimes asking a constituent nicely for a bribe didn't work. For those especially stubborn cases, there was always blackmail and extortion to fall back on.

In addition to all of this bribery and extortion going on, there were also problems with the way taxes were collected, especially during the time of the Roman Empire. Of course, the Romans needed public money to build practical things like the sewers and aqueducts, and also for fun things, like the arenas and amphitheaters. So, to collect the money it needed, ancient Rome developed a system of taxes.

During the early days of the Republic, taxes were modest, ranging from only one to three percent. Taxes would be levied in those days on the value of land, homes, animals, and other possessions. Later on though, when the Empire was established and as it expanded across three continents, much more money was needed. So, the Roman Empire established a system of tax collectors called tax farmers.

A tax farmer would purchase the rights from the Roman Senate to tax people in a particular jurisdiction. This practice might have only caused a little bit of corruption, but the real problems came about because the Senate didn't put any controls whatsoever on the tax farmers. The Senate failed to specify tedious things like what assets or income should be taxed, or what the tax rate was, or who should be taxed. All of those small, little details were worked out by the tax farmer. Of course, many of the tax farmers got greedy and demanded much more in tax, or even in bribes, than what could have been considered fair. And don't forget that the tax farmers wielded a kind of absolute power because you could be sold into slavery in ancient Rome if you didn't pay your taxes. So, like running for public office, being a tax collector was big business in those days.

With all of this corruption going on, there were eventually so many people trying to get into public office that there was a political frenzy. Certain laws had been passed in the intervening years to try to control the situation, but breaking them had few if any consequences, and as a result, the attempted controls had very little effect. Around 40 BC, a much stricter law was finally established that set out severe punishments for both the briber and the bribee. What was the punishment? Ten years in exile.

Although extreme, this law came too late in the day to bring about any real change. Political corruption had already been established as the norm, and elections were often rigged, right through the time of the Empire. For those who craved power and status and had the wealth and connections to do so, it was easy just to pay for the votes they needed. And over time, as more and more wealthy and powerful men came into public office, the needs of the common person were quickly forgotten.

In this way, graft and corruption were rife throughout the Republic and the Empire. Of course, this had an effect on larger society because if you saw that the wealthy and powerful were getting what they wanted by unfair means, why not just join the party yourself? Remember that there was no such thing as a police force in those days. So, crime started to be a real problem. Traveling alone was especially precarious, and solo travelers were sometimes kidnapped and sold into slavery. It was at this point that life started to become a bit messy and difficult.

With crime on the rise, the punishment of those committing crimes became a much more urgent issue. Nevertheless, the punishment for committing a crime was not the same for everyone, and this is where the true perils of failing to live as a responsible member of Roman society became especially evident. Instead of the punishment fitting the crime, the punishment had to fit your social status. So, a wealthy person would get a much less severe punishment for the same offense than a poor person, a non-citizen would get worse treatment than a citizen, and slaves would get the worst treatment by far. [16]

Torture was often considered a practical way to extract information from prisoners in those days. If you were a slave, you had to be subjected to mandatory torture in order for your testimony to be admissible in court. For anyone else, if you refused to speak, you were probably tortured just as a matter of routine, because of course, there would have to be some evidence to corroborate or refute in court.

Most crimes were tried in court quickly, and punishment was meted out very swiftly after judgement had been pronounced. However, people weren't sentenced to prison in those days for the crimes they committed. That's simply because the ancient Romans didn't believe in anything as forward-thinking or optimistic as rehabilitation, neither during the Republic nor during the Empire. The purpose of prisons was for those awaiting trial or punishment, and in order to prevent escape during the time they were waiting, prisoners might have had to wear a cumbersome pair of heavy wooden shoes.

Punishments could range anywhere from a fine to death, depending on the accused's social status, as well as the severity of the offense. Apart from fines, whipping and public flogging were the most common punishments. If sentenced to death, it could either be a slow or hasty one. For the slow death route, a person might have had to do hard labor in a quarry for a number of years until they died from exhaustion or they might even have been forced to fight as a gladiator.

For the speedy death route, there were various forms of capital punishment. Executions were carried out in public, so they had to be crowd pleasers. In order to please the crowd, punishments were deliberately designed to be as agonizing as possible to ensure a good day's entertainment. The public was so blasé about capital punishment in those days that they could even get motifs of execution scenes to hang up in their houses for decoration.

Those sentenced to death could be beheaded, thrown into a river, flung over the edge of a cliff, fed to beasts, or even buried alive. Being killed by crucifixion was one of the most feared punishments, although this form of retribution was usually reserved for those who had committed treason. If you were a citizen, however, you could ask to be beheaded instead of crucified, so citizenship really did come with its advantages. A truly special and ingenious punishment awaited those who had committed the second-most heinous crime: parricide. If you killed your parent or an elder relative, you would first be flogged in public before being sewn into a sack that contained a viper, a rooster, a dog, and a monkey.

Since punishments were so horrid and because they were usually carried out in public, prisoners often tried to commit suicide first. And if you were an upper-class prisoner, you might have even been offered that option as an opportunity to save face.

You may take all of the talk of corruption and crime and punishment in this chapter to mean that life in ancient Rome was a pretty stern, joyless affair. But that's really far from true. After all, one of life's greatest joys was widely and abundantly available in ancient Rome. What was that pleasure? Wine.

Chapter 7 – Wine

Wine was a very important commodity in ancient Rome, although it's difficult to say with certainty when it started to be produced there. That's because grapevines grew naturally in Italy for centuries without any cultivation before wine started to be made. However, the first real evidence that we have of wine being produced was around 800 BC in the Italian Province of Tuscany.

Winemaking seems to have been at its best during the Roman Empire in the second century AD, when vineyards were planted near larger cities like Naples and Venice. The best estimates of wine consumption at that time are that each Roman citizen was drinking around one bottle of wine per day, with 180 million quarts of wine being consumed in total across the Empire.

That may sound excessive, but in ancient Rome, wine really was a basic daily necessity. The Romans even had a deity called Bacchus that was devoted to the reverence and worship of the beverage. Wine was available to persons from any social class, including slaves. For example, in the second century BC, Cato the Elder proposed that slaves should be given 260 quarts of wine per year.

With slaves being one of the more disadvantaged classes of Roman society, we can only assume that the consumption of wine for the average person was much greater than this. Of course, wine became better throughout the Republic and especially as the Empire developed, which probably increased the demand for the beverage. One estimate indicates that the average consumption of wine at the end of the Empire was probably closer to three quarts per day.

Also, wine was very affordable in those days, so it was drunk every day at home. It would be drunk with meals. It would even be quaffed with something as simple as a little bit of bread. Men and women also had it at banquets, if they were invited or if they could afford to host them. But at these banquets, the quality of the wine you got was determined by your social class. That meant that the best wine was saved for the most prestigious guests, while guests of lesser importance got the dregs.

Nonetheless, holding a banquet was an expensive undertaking that many people would not have been able to enjoy. The plebian population would have consumed much of their wine in taverns, shoulder to shoulder with slaves and prostitutes. As you can imagine, with such a colorful cast of characters and adding alcohol into the mix, fights and even riots would sometimes break out.

So, how did the Romans manage to produce such extensive quantities of this essential beverage? Well, they had to start at the very beginning in the early days of the Roman Kingdom by determining which types of soil and climates would best support the growth of particular types of grapes. They quickly realized that the vines needed to be propped up as they grew in order to keep the fruit off the ground, so they developed special trellises for that purpose. In addition, they understood that the vines had to be pruned regularly to promote the health and growth of the grapes that were being produced.

Once the grapes were produced and harvested, they actually were stomped on by foot, as is often depicted in movies that portray ancient Rome. Slaves were usually the ones to perform this tedious and often foot-staining task. Then the mixture, called must, was placed into a winepress. The juice flowed out of the winepress into a pool, where slaves dipped it out and put it into large clay pots.

Probably because of the demand for wine, these pots were really very large; they would have usually held somewhere around twenty-five gallons of wine each, so the logistics of handling them needed to be considered carefully. Normally these pots would have first been lined with beeswax to seal off the porousness of the clay. The pots were then buried up to their necks in the ground. This was both to protect them as well as to promote aging and fermentation. Once the wine was fermented, it would be transferred to one of beautiful Roman containers called an amphora, where it was left until it was ready to be drunk.

The whole process from pressing to serving usually took about six weeks, but the really good stuff would be left a lot longer, even up to twenty years for the highest quality wines. Much of the wine produced in ancient Rome would have been very boozy white wine, although red wines, which were reported to sometimes produce severe hangovers, were also available. And although most wine was drunk at room temperature, the elite would have chilled their wine in pits that were lined with straw and then filled with snow.

So, we know that there were different types and qualities of wine in those days, and a small fraction of it would have been aged to near perfection for the elite who could afford it. However, the majority of it would have been downright nasty and probably tasted more like vinegar. To get around this problem, the ever-resourceful Romans had a solution. Way ahead of their Prohibition era descendants, the Romans would just add more stuff to their wine to disguise the nasty taste.

They would add honey or must juice from the press to make the wine sweet. In order to enhance sweetness further, they also, unfortunately, sometimes added lead though, which is now known to be highly toxic. They would also add spices like fennel, thyme, and pepper to make the wine palatable, and eventually these herbs were added during fermentation so that the flavors would better infuse into the liquid.

Some of the mixers could get pretty exotic. For example, let's look at Cato the Elder in the second century BC. Perhaps wanting to rival an ancient Greek predecessor from many centuries earlier named Homer, whose favorite drink was made of wine, honey, goat's cheese, and barley meal, Cato is said to have added a pinch of marble dust and a drop of pig's blood to his tipple.

In addition to these libations, there was something called new wine. This would have been wine that had had a brief fermentation period – anywhere from six to twenty-one days. At that point in the fermentation process, the wine basically would have been a foamy liquid that was about twelve percent alcohol, and it only could have been kept on hand for ten days before it turned rancid.

Nevertheless, many people consumed and enjoyed new wine in those days, much like we enjoy sweet cider nowadays.

Also bear in mind that wine was almost never consumed without first mixing in quite a lot of water. It just would have been too potent and really quite unpalatable on its own. Normally, you'd have about three parts water to one part wine in your favorite drinking vessel. With all of the sweeteners and herbs in the wine, not to mention water that was added, the resulting concoction would have tasted something like the spiked punch that you might have imbibed upon at your senior prom. In contrast, if you were lucky enough to attend a banquet, you would have had your wine mixed just for you, to your taste, in your own drinking vessel. [17]

Besides the taste, there were other reasons why water was added to wine. Undiluted wine was very highly alcoholic, and mixing it with water meant that it was far less likely to make a person drunk, which of course, helped to reduce public intoxication. In those days, the wine was also cleaner and safer to drink than much of the water was. So, the wine not only improved the taste of the water, but was believed to actually purify it.

Since many of the wines in those days had herbs added to them, the Romans who lived during the time of the Republic and throughout the Empire also believed that the beverage had true medicinal properties and that drinking it was good for you. As the Empire grew, it was mandatory for Roman soldiers to drink around a quart of wine every day in the belief that it would fortify them and keep them fit and well.

In Roman culture then, drinking wine was a very common and widespread practice, and consuming the beverage was not only limited to forts, taverns, and private homes. The elite would even drink theirs in sensual, beautiful venues like gardens. [18]

What all of this means is that, really, everybody was a drinker in those days, throughout the time of the Republic through to the end of the Empire. And as there was a Roman god for wine, the Romans had a high regard for the beverage. Its virtues were extolled in songs and poems of the day, and conversation seemed to flow whenever the drink was consumed. For some, wine was regarded as life's greatest pleasure and as a pleasure that was known to heighten other pleasures! For example, the tombstone of one Flavius Agricola, located just outside of Rome, reads: "Friends, listen to my advice. Mix wine, then place garlands around your head, and drink deep. And do not deny the beautiful girls the sweets of your love."

As another Italian you may have heard of called Verdi wrote many centuries later in his opera, *La Traviata*: "Let's drink. Drink from the joyful chalices since beauty is blossoming. Let's drink among those sweet quivers that love makes arise, since the eye goes to one's almighty heart. Let's drink, my love, so that our love among the chalices will bring hotter kisses." In any event . . . these verses remind us that it's been known from time immemorial that wine can make "sexy time" a lot more fun and enjoyable.

Since going to the baths was another enjoyable experience, and one where a person could enjoy certain other pleasures of the flesh by paying a bit extra to get a prostitute, wine was also carried into the bath houses and consumed there. Echoing the thoughts of our friend Flavius Agricola, the epitaph of another Roman called Tiberius Claudius Secundus states that "baths, wine, and sex corrupt out bodies, but baths, wine, and sex make life worth living." Yet, it does seem that not everyone was on board with all of these pleasures of the flesh. In the second century BC, Pliny the Elder commented on the perils associated with insobriety, as did the scholar Seneca in the first century AD. A particular lament was the fact that some bathers didn't know how to go home from the baths sober. [19]

But let's not go overboard with all of this talk of drinking and bathing and sex. One cannot assume, dear reader, that what the ancient Romans really liked was a good orgy. Yes, it's true. Although all forms of debauchery are usually depicted in movies about Roman Emperors, who, like Caligula, were actually a bit partial to having a raging orgy or two at his banquets, this was far, far from the norm for most Romans.

Of course, it's difficult to talk about sexual morality in ancient Rome, which covers a time span of more than a thousand years. That would be like us comparing today's values to those of the tenth century, after all. However, what we can say with some certainty is that the idea that most Romans were promiscuous and debauched is massively erroneous. That's because the Romans followed a set of moral guidelines that idealized self-control for men, chastity for women, and the avoidance of sexual excess for people of all genders. In addition to these unwritten norms, there were laws about sexual offenses in ancient Rome. For instance, rape was illegal and could carry a death sentence, and children were also protected against sexual violence.

Still, some members of the populace were afforded very little protection. Consider the case of prostitutes. Prostitution was not just legal; it was commonplace in those days. But working girls needed to engage in their craft at their own risk. Prostitutes were given no protection against rape, and were expected just to accept whatever abuse they got. In much the same way, slaves couldn't be raped, because after all, they were considered property rather than people. All of this meant that men could consider women working as prostitutes, or even as dancing girls, to be fair game, and these women were left without any protection at all. [20]

But enough of all of this talk of sex. There are other pleasures that one can enjoy with wine, like a good feast. And the wall paintings in Pompeii certainly help to promote the stereotype of Roman dining as a hedonistic indulgence. One scene, for example, shows two couples reclining on couches with wine on tables nearby. It can be assumed from the scene that a good deal of drinking has already taken place at this party. That's because, in the background of the image, there is another man who has passed out and a woman who is being propped up by her slave. In another scene, we can see a slave mixing wine with water in a large bowl. In yet another, one of the guests is already so drunk that he is throwing up.

But although the stereotype of the average Roman being a glutton and a drunkard is false, it is true that the really wealthy Romans did enjoy a good feast. Such occasions would have been complete with entertainment, like dancers and musicians, but the food and wine were really the main attractions. Recipes discovered from the time of ancient Rome show that Romans, especially during the time of the Empire, enjoyed elaborate and lavish presentations of food, like meats stuffed inside other meats. What the Roman upper class especially loved was a dish called turducken. This consisted of a roast chicken inside a roast duck inside a roast turkey. [21]

So, is it true that Romans would throw up after a big meal so that they could carry on eating more? If you have heard of the vomitorium, you might think that bulimia was rampant in ancient Rome. This myth of excess and gluttony has made its way into quite a few books and movies now. But again, it is far from the truth. [22]

Okay, it's no wonder that after consuming a feast that might have consisted of plentiful wine and stuffed meats, not to mention delicacies like sow's udder, Syrian dates, and lobster, a Roman diner might have felt uncomfortably full. However, research tells us that while a few of the Emperors did actually vomit between courses, the idea that participants at a banquet chucked up after eating is nothing but sheer myth. Above all, they wouldn't have wanted to waste that luscious chicken-inside-a-duck-inside-a-turkey, and they just wouldn't have been that unappreciative of the economic value of the food they had been served, let alone intentionally wasting the calories that they had consumed. [23]

So, Romans did know very well the joys of drinking and bathing and sex and eating. And when they had their fill of all of these delights, there was yet one more exciting activity that they could try their hands at: travel.

Chapter 8 – Roadways and Travel

Speaking of travel, you may well have heard the expression "All roads lead to Rome." But what is the origin of this phrase? Well, as the Republic began to expand in its early days, it soon became evident that a system was needed to move goods and people in and around the capital. Enter Appius Claudius Caecus, who worked as a censor, which was something like a magistrate in charge of public finance. He ordered that work begin on a roadway system, without even having had this approved by the Senate. After all, he had been responsible for the plans for the Appia Aqueduct, which had been a huge success, and he literally wanted to build his legacy in the city of Rome. So, work began on the Via Appia in 312 BC.

This road was really important, especially on a strategic level. On it, military troops could travel to any number of locations around the Republic. Essential supplies could also be transported to military bases and forts. Before construction started on the Via Appia, there were only a handful of roads that led out of the capital, and they were in really poor condition. So, it had been extremely difficult to move soldiers and weapons to the battlefront without facing severe impediments from the terrain and from the enemy.

The movement of troops and supplies was essential in 312 BC when construction on the road started because the Romans were at war against the Samnites, a group of rebels from southern Italy. With the Via Appia completed, the Romans quelled the Samnites, and Roman rule really started to flourish.

Besides the battle against the Samnites, many other historically significant events took place on or along the Via Appia. You've certainly heard of the famous gladiator named Spartacus. Well, he led a revolt with six thousand slaves in 73 BC called the Third Servile War. The rebellion was called this because it was the third and last revolt led by slaves against the Romans. When the Roman military eventually captured Spartacus in a trap that they had set in 71 BC, they crucified him and killed all of the slave rebels, and it is said that nearly six thousand bodies lined the Via Appia after the battle.

Speaking of those who were crucified, it is also said that the Via Appia was traveled by none other than Jesus Christ from 30 AD to 33 AD as he preached and spread his message. Because the Via Appia was the way to travel out of Rome, many other famous people would have traveled on it, including all of the Roman rulers and emperors, and many important historical events took place on it.

However, the Via Appia, which extended from Rome to Brindisi in southern Italy, wasn't the only Roman road, of course. By the time the Empire fell in 476 AD, the Romans had built roads that extended to three continents – covering Europe, including Great Britain, the Middle East, and north Africa. In the end, there were twenty-nine roads altogether, and they were 5,600 miles total in length. This was really a vast network of roads, and they connected all 113 parts of the Empire to Rome itself. Hence the expression: All roads lead to Rome. And since the roadway system was so extensive, there was also something called the *itinerarium*, which was a list of destinations along the roads that extended to the borders of the Roman domain.

So, we know that the roadways were extensive and that many well-known figures traveled on them. But VIP's weren't the only ones to use the roadways. That's simply because people and supplies needed to come into the capital, in addition to people and supplies going out of it. This leads to the next question: Exactly who else and what else was moving on these roads?

Well, Rome was a busy, growing metropolis. It had become very cosmopolitan with many foreign residents as the Empire grew – they came mainly from Greece, Judea, and northern Africa – and it's estimated that there were over a million inhabitants in Rome when the Empire fell. That's a lot of people, especially when considering the how limited the available technologies would have been, even as late as the fifth century.

What did a growing population like this need? Food and workers. So, the roadways were also used to transport slaves up from northern Africa and other parts of the Empire. The bulk of the grain for the most important foodstuff, bread, also came from northern Africa, but any other supply you can imagine, from olive oil, to wine, to cloth and dyes and beyond were carried along these roadway systems. Of course, don't forget the military, who would bring more slaves and any other spoils of war back into the capital.

You may wonder, who else was traveling on these roads? Well, there was a small toll for any non-official traveler to use the roadways, so there was a small cost associated with travel, but there were travelers of all sorts on these roads, from the rich to poor, the law-abiding to thugs, and the clean to the smelly. Messengers like the American Pony Express also ran along these roads to deliver missives, and they could travel up to sixty miles each day to reach their destinations. Some travelers managed distances even farther than this. For instance, it is said that as early as 9 BC, Emperor

Tiberius traveled 215 miles within a 24-hour period to get to his dying brother.

With these relatively large distances being traveled, you might be tempted to think that the journey was easy and comfortable. But compared to our modern-day standards, that really wasn't the case. It is true though, that the Romans were real masters of construction for their time, and part of their mastery involved building their roads as straight as they possibly could. This was done for two reasons. First of all, it made the distances between destinations as short as possible, making it more efficient to move people and supplies around, especially for military purposes. Secondly, winding roads meant more places to hide, so straight roads helped to cut down on the problem of banditry. That's because there was an improved line of sight on a straight road.

The Romans also realized that rain, and consequently mud, really impeded travel, so they used a very special, and quite advanced method to construct the roads. The first job when building the road was to clear the path, especially of rocks and foliage. This task was performed by soldiers who had been assign to the road construction crew. Next, they would dig out where the road was going to be placed and fill this in with the largest stones they could find.

After that they put in pebbles, sand, and cement, and compacted it all down. On top of this base, they put broken tiles for drainage, and then finally, the construction was topped off with tightly-fitting paving stones that made up the surface of the road. They ensured that the road sloped down on both sides from the middle so that water would drain away. Finally, they put in curbstones to hold everything together. The curbs also formed a channel where the water would flow away from the surface of the road.

But while these construction methods did help with drainage, the road surface itself was cobbled and, as a result, very bumpy. For this reason, horse-driven chariots were not as common on the roads as you might have thought. The wooden wheels on the chariot would have made for a very jarring ride as the wheels rolled over the cobbles, so some Emperors would have been carried on something called a litter. You've probably seen these in movies – they are a chair attached to two horizontal poles, carried by two slaves at the front and two at the back. Although this was mode of transport was much, much slower than traveling by chariot, it was much more comfortable and, of course, appeared more stately and imposing to any onlookers. Obviously, not everyone could travel in such style though. Besides these regal travelers, there also would have been people on horseback and plenty of people just walking.

With all of these people moving around, how did the Romans make the roads safe? Well, besides making the roads straight for good visibility, the military was deployed to patrol the roads during the age of the Empire. We know that around the time of Spartacus in the first century BC, robbery on the roadways was an ever-present peril. Research shows that, during the days of the Empire at least, soldiers were sent out to catch thieves, and that members of the militia were even killed by attacking bandits.

To address this problem, a system was established whereby other soldiers, known as the *stationarii* and *beneficiarii*, would take up posts in watchtowers. To protect as many travelers as possible, these military watchmen were sent to both well-traveled and remote locations. After all, protection was needed on the less-traveled roads where travelers were often the most vulnerable to attack. The watchmen not only collected any tolls that were due, they also had to be on the lookout for run-away slaves and help pass off messages to those Pony-Express-style messengers, who relayed them to their final destinations.

But even though tolls were being collected, they were fairly modest, and more income needed to be collected to aid in the project of expanding the infrastructure of the Empire. So, besides collecting tolls, the Romans also imposed duties on the goods that were being conveyed along the roadway systems. The troops would assess the value of the goods being carried, levy a fee, and collect the taxes that were due. This usually occurred at significant landmarks, such as bridges, borders of provinces, or mountain passes.

In spite of the presence of the military in these watchtowers, robbery still sometimes took place on the roads throughout the Empire. For example, during the time of Emperor Commodus, from 176 to 180 AD, there was a problem with bandits in the Roman outpost of Gaul, a region that we know today as the country of France. A gang of robbers traveling through Gaul had all sorts of mayhem on their minds. Not only were they robbing and pillaging as much as they could, they also intended to assassinate the Emperor, and obviously, this uprising had to be quelled. Several years later, there was also a well-recorded case involving a problem with gangs of bandits in the south of Italy, which also had to be dealt with.

We can't really be sure about the full extent of the problem though, because research on these banditry episodes is a little bit sketchy. One of the reasons that it's difficult to assess the problem with certainty is because we know that the military would sometimes be pulled away from their outposts and watchtowers to fight in military campaigns or perform other more pressing duties. However, we do know that the most wealthy would have traveled with multiple escorts or even with a sizeable security entourage. We also know that armed force sometimes had to be used to suppress bandits and that sometimes fatalities occurred as a result.

With the volume of traffic, not the mention the battles and deaths occurring on the roadways, something had to be done with the remains of those who passed away. Perhaps predictably then, there are several burial sites and catacombs lining these roadways, especially on the Via Appia. These cemeteries also grew because burials were not permitted within the city walls of Rome. So, burial sites sprung into existence, especially around the outskirts of the capital.

After they were dead and gone, you would get your loved one the most elaborate tomb or headstone that money could buy. The inscriptions on many of these grave markers were very extensive and elaborate because the survivors wanted to extol the life and virtues of the deceased. And funerals quickly became big business, especially around the capital.

Funeral processions, especially those leading out of Rome, were grand affairs, complete with professional mourners. After all, nothing else publicized how important your dearly departed was than hiring a throng of strangers to cry and wail. In an ancient example of "keeping up with the Joneses," these processions increasingly grew in size, and the processions eventually got so large that laws were passed to limit the number of professional mourners that could be present at a funeral.

So, we know that the roadways could be uncomfortable and dangerous, even to the point of causing fatalities, and that traveling took a lot of time. Because of this, many journeys would have been long, drawn-out affairs, so the travelers needed stopovers to rest for the night.

In order to fulfil this need, the Romans laid out a substantial number of roadside inns and post houses on the road network. In addition, there were liveries or stables to accommodate horses and donkeys. Official travelers for the government who needed to travel quickly, like messengers and tax collectors, could even leave their animals there to rest, and get a fresh, unwinded one for the remainder of their journeys. Since animals needed to be rested frequently, these stables and liveries were situated every ten miles along many of the roads.

Wherever there was a livery, there would also be a roadside inn for weary travelers. These were essentially state-run hotels and way stations where travelers could get a drink, a meal, and retire for the evening. The most ubiquitous of these were called *mutationes*, which were basic houses with a bed for the night and stables for animals, but no further facilities.

In addition, there were more elaborate arrangements called *mansiones* about every twenty miles. A *mansion* had lodgings for animals and travelers, as well as food, baths, and repair stations for wagons . . . not to mention prostitutes.

With this motley crew of various travelers, little wonder that the stopover experience could range from the sketchy to the downright seedy. The average traveler would have had to put up with bad wine, dirty water, and poor service. [24] Horace, in the first century BC, expresses what quite a few travelers must have experienced in the following satirical description of a journey from Rome:

"We slow-pokes had to split up our journey, even though the best travelers could get to their destinations in one day. The Via Appia is better if you take it slowly. At our stop for the night, the water was so awful that it declared war with my stomach. Then I had to wait in a foul mood for the rest of my companions to finish their meal while the night cast its shadows over the sky."

His description of a later stopover is even more colorful: "I stupidly lay awake until midnight waiting for a girl who never came. My sleep was driven by Venus, and full of unclean visions, I soiled my nightdress while sleeping." [25]

So, from this sort of literature, we can really get the full flavor of the stopovers along the Roman roadways. And although these venues may have started off as small stopovers, they developed and grew over time, sometimes becoming thriving metropolises in themselves. For example, London, Budapest, Belgrade, and Istanbul all started off as simple outposts on Roman roads.

THE END

Sources and Further Reading

[1] Monty Python. *Monty Python's Life of Brian*, 1979, HandMade Films.

[2] Chelsea Wald. "Ancient Rome's Terrorizing Toilets," *Discover Magazine*, June 2014.

[3] Piers Mitchell. "Roman Toilets Gave No Clear Health Benefit and Romanisation Actually Spread Parasites." *Parasitology*, Jan. 2016. Cambridge University.

[4] Ann Olga Koloski-Ostrow. "Talking Heads: What Toilets and Sewers Tell Us about Ancient Roman Sanitation." *The Conversation*, Nov. 2015.

[5] Steve Muench. "Water and the Development of Ancient Rome." *We're Never Far from Where We Were*, Jan. 2018.

[6] E. J. Dembskey. "Aqua Appia." *Roman Aqueducts: Rome Aqua Appia (Italy)*, 2009.

[7] Roger D. Hansen. "Water and Wastewater Systems in Imperial Rome," *Water History*, 2021.

[8] Andrew Wilson. Water, Power, and Culture in the Roman and Byzantine Worlds: An Introduction," Mar. 2012. Oxford University.

[9] Mary Beard. *Meet the Romans with Mary Beard*. 2012. Film. BBC.

[10] John Byron Kuhner. "Of Cabbages and Kings." [extracted from Cato, Agr., 160]; Eidolon, May 2015.

[11] Jane Draycott. "Flower Power: Cato's Medicinal Recipes," *The Recipes Project: Food, Magic, Art, Science, and Medicine*, Jan. 2015.

[12] Meghan E. Wooster. "Escape from a Greater Affliction: The Historical Evolution of Amputation," Feb. 2012. Des Moines University, and Jane Draycott. "Severed Limbs and Wounded Feet: How the Ancients Invented Prosthetics," *The Independent*. May 2017.

[13] Oliver J. Thatcher, ed., "The Library of Original Sources" (Milwaukee: University Research Extension Co., 1907), Vol. III: The Roman World.

[14] Harold Whetstone Johnston. "The Private Life of the Romans" Revised by Mary Johnston. Scott, Foresman and Company, 1932.

[15] William C. Morey, Ph.D., D.C.L. *Outlines of Roman History*. New York, American Book Company, 1901.

[16] Ducksters. "Ancient Rome: Roman Law." Jan. 2021.

[17] Katharine Raff, "The Roman Banquet" *Heilbrunn Timeline of Art History* Metropolitan Museum of Art, Oct. 2011.

[18] Stuart Fleming "VINUM: *The Story of Roman Wine*. Glen Mills, PA, Art Flair, 2001.

[19] Carla Raimer. "Ancient Worlds: Ancient Roman Recipes." PBS. Nov. 2000.

[20] Colin Ricketts. Promiscuity in Antiquity: Sex in Ancient Rome. *History Hit.* Jan 2021.

[21] Stephane Pappas. "What's a Vomitorum?" *Live Science.* Aug. 2016.

[22] Stephanie Pappas. "Purging the Myth of the Vomitorium." *Scientific American.* Aug. 2016.

[23] Cillan Davenport and Shushma Malik. "Mythbusting Ancient Rome." *The Conversation.* Jan. 2017.

[24] Mark Cartwright. "Roman Roads." *World History Encyclopedia.* Sep. 2014.

[25] Erik Jensen. "The Road to Peace: Horace's Fifth Satire as Travel Literature." 2013. University of Illinois. Excerpted from Horatius Flaccus (Horace) Satires 1.5.

NOTES: